Gifts of the Journey

Gifts of the Journey

A Journey to Forgiveness, Love and Hope

Allen Rowe

iUniverse, Inc.
New York Lincoln Shanghai

Gifts of the Journey
A Journey to Forgiveness, Love and Hope

iUniverse, Inc.

For information address:
iUniverse, Inc.
2021 Pine Lake Road, Suite 100
Lincoln, NE 68512
www.iuniverse.com

ISBN: 0-595-31228-4

Printed in the United States of America

CONTENTS

ACKNOWLEDGEMENTS

There are so many people and events who have played an important role in helping this book come to life.

I am grateful for the tough times along the way and the lessons each one of these situations has taught me on this journey we call life. It is from these experiences I was shaped and molded like a piece of potter's clay.

I am forever indebted to my dear grandmother, Mamaw, who left this world many years ago for a better place. Mamaw and her love remain with me today. The foundation she provided me as a child has guided me through life and kept me strong when times were tough.

I am blessed for the love of my two daughters, Kristi and Angela. We have been through so much together and each day I cherish them more. They have each given me so much in their own unique way and I love them more than they will ever know.

For the many people who have touched my life and heart over the past fifty plus years, who have shown kindness, provided guidance and been there as friends—thank you.

Finally I would like to thank my best friend, partner and soul mate—my wife Clarissa. Her love, support, cheerleading and sweetness of spirit has touched my heart and soul like never before. She has taught me the joy and beauty of pure love and I thank God for her each and every day.

INTRODUCTION

What began as a sad time in my life became a journey toward personal transformation. This pilgrimage of the heart has proven to be a powerful process of self-examination, healing, and forgiveness—and is ongoing today.

Gifts of the Journey is a tale of a little boy whose early years were filled with the love of a grandmother, and then without warning, his world and life was turned upside down. And so his journey began. Along the way there were dark times and periods in his life. His journey took him through many of the same challenges you may have faced, or are facing, in your life.

As the little boy grew into a man he came to terms with his past, understood his purpose in life, the power of forgiveness—and discovered the gifts he now shares with the world.

The internationally recognized expert on relationships, Dr. Barbara De Angelis says "everyone comes into our lives for a reason—to teach us a lesson and allow us to grow." There is a reason this book is now in your hands. Perhaps now is the time chosen in your life for you to learn certain lessons necessary for your personal growth. There is a reason this time has come *now* not sooner. Lessons are only learned when the time is right. My purpose is to share with you the hope of a new tomorrow, a rebirth of your soul, and the gifts you can share with the world in a way you feel comfortable with.

1

CHAPTER 1

Not Like Everyone Else

From his earliest memories the little boy felt different from everyone else. Without a mother or father he wasn't like other kids at school. In an era of Ozzie & Harriet families instead of growing up with parents he lived with aging grandparents, having been sent to them as an infant. Although they tried, and he loved them so, they were not the Mom and Dad he longed for as a child.

In time the little boy realized he would never enjoy the special love of a mother or father, or a parent's wise counsel from childhood to adulthood. He would never have a father teach him to throw a baseball or cheer from the sidelines at a Little League game. He would never have a mother to hold him when he was sick, or dote over him before his first prom. Sadly because of this, he would never be able to return love to aging parents, to care for and comfort them in the sunset of their lives.

Because of this void in his life, the little boy felt disconnected and lonely. To make matters worse, his early childhood brought many sad events, beginning with the death of his Uncle Bob.

Uncle Bob was a police officer and his hero. On one occasion Uncle Bob took him to the city jail. As he held Uncle Bob's hand

and walked through the jail, prisoners called out "Mr. Bob! Mr. Bob!" Bob would stop and talk with them, his gentle voice asking how their Momma or Daddy was doing. Many of the inmates were black. In a time when the Klan was alive and well in America, this was an unusual sight. Whites & blacks did not mix—but Uncle Bob didn't worry about all that. He just cared.

The little boy admired Uncle Bob like the father he wished for—but soon this strong man was gone and the circumstances of his death would haunt the little boy for many years.

We've all experienced difficult times in our lives, and it doesn't matter what caused the tough times or pain. Pain is pain regardless of what caused it, or how deep it's wounds. It just plain hurts.

The painful events in our lives and their origin are different for each of us. The pain you live with today may be rooted in events from your childhood. Perhaps you lived in a violent home where your parents fought constantly. You may have suffered physical or sexual abuse. Perhaps you were taunted by other kids because you were a different color, had a deformity, or wore tattered hand-me-down clothes to school because your parents were poor. For others your pain may stem from illness, a divorce, or the loss of a lover, parent, or sibling.

As a child you may have felt you were different or not as good as others, that something was wrong with you. You may not have understood at the time, or even today, the impact of these events on your life. We've all had our own cross to bear, so to speak.

I can still picture myself as a child standing in my grandmother's living room in Monahans, Texas. From the window,

I watched, as my buddy next door wrestled and laughed with his father on their lawn. I remember being angry but also sad that I didn't have a Dad to wrestle with. More than once I thought maybe I didn't have a Dad because there was something "wrong" with me.

Moments like these pass, but the memories can haunt us for years, as they did me. The deep emotional scars of childhood have a way of coming back into our lives during our journey through life. Some are able to come to terms with the scars of their past while others are destroyed by them. You've probably known examples of both.

What are the scars of your past? Have you tucked them away in a deep, hidden chamber of your heart to forget them? Perhaps for you they're more alive than dead. Maybe they aren't scars at all—rather still open, unhealed wounds after all these years.

In her book, *Something More*, Sarah Ban Breathnach tells us, "*We don't have to be, become, or stay, victims of circumstances forever unless we choose to do so. We are meant to live through our circumstances—not stay stuck in them.*"

My hope for you is that from this day forward you will begin your own personal journey of understanding, healing and forgiveness.

You may be comfortable with the thought of trying to understand your past and allowing yourself to heal—but forgiveness for some of you may be a little too much to ask. I understand. It took me a long time too.

Perhaps your pain was caused by someone who betrayed your trust, someone who caused you great physical or emotional distress. Because of this, forgiveness may seem impossible to you, but it is absolutely necessary if you want to dispose of the emotional baggage you've been dragging behind you all these years. The depth of your pain or anger may seem too great, or that your tormentors don't deserve forgiveness.

The late Dr. Lewis Smedes, professor emeritus at the Fuller Seminary, in his book, *Forgive and Forget: Healing the Wounds We Don't Deserve*, says; *"If we say monsters are beyond forgiving, we give them a power they should never have. Monsters who are too evil to be forgiven get a stranglehold on their victims; they can sentence their victims to a lifetime of unhealed pain."*

"They are given power to keep their evil alive in the hearts of those who suffered most. Forgiveness in no way absolves one of the responsibility for what they did to you. Refusal to forgive however means that until you do, you will forever hold on to the stuff related to the pain inflicted on you."

We weren't meant to become slaves to our past and the monsters who have hurt us. I thought I knew all about forgiveness, but I eventually realized I had a lot to learn about letting go and moving on.

Dr. Fred Luskin points out in his wonderful book, *Forgive for Good,*

"Forgiveness is for you and not the offender"

"Forgiveness is taking back your power"

"Forgiveness is taking responsibility for how you feel"

"Forgiveness is about your healing and not the people who hurt you"

"Forgiveness is becoming a hero not a victim"

"Forgiveness is a choice"

I finally realized forgiving was a way to set myself free from the past, to take back my power and gain the inner strength and peace I longed for. In Dr. Luskin's book I also learned what forgiveness was not. Dr. Luskin tells us that:

"Forgiveness is not condoning unkindness"

"Forgiveness is not forgetting that something painful happened"

"Forgiveness is not excusing poor behavior"

"Forgiveness is not denying or minimizing your hurt"

"Forgiveness does not mean reconciling with the offender"

"Forgiveness does not mean you give up having feelings"

During my law enforcement career I've dealt with many people who were horribly wronged. Parents who've lost a child to senseless gang violence, spouses abused by their partners, children betrayed and abused by parents or other relatives. Some moved on with their lives while others seemed to slowly self-destruct. Had I known more about the power of forgiveness at the time, I might have been able to make a difference in their lives.

For myself, I know that when I finally learned to forgive those who had caused me such pain in my life, a tremendous sense of peace came over me. I could almost feel the poison drain from my soul.

CHAPTER 2

Stranger at the Door

"Who is this lady?" the little boy wondered as he looked up at her tense, weathered face. Even as a boy he could sense she was not a nice lady. Maybe it was her jet-black hair, the scowl on her face, or the way she talked. Her name was Jean and she was his grandmother's daughter—and his mother.

She told Mamaw she was taking him with her. "How could she do this?" he thought as he stood behind Mamaw clinging to her dress. He had been with Mamaw almost since birth. Without warning, or time to get to know him, the stranger had suddenly appeared one afternoon to take him away from the only home he had ever known. Although his older sister lived with his Mom, he was afraid.

In fear the little boy ran. Out the back door of Mamaw's tiny home in Wickett, Texas, across the road and into an open field. He ran as fast as he could, crying as he went. He was scared to death. He did not want to leave Mamaw. Uncle Bob and Papaw were both gone now, and if he left, Mamaw would be all alone. Who would take care of her?

As he ran he heard footsteps behind him and his cousin Billy calling out to him. Billy caught up with him, consoled him, and managed to get the little boy back to the house. Before he could protest further, he was in the back of the stranger's car. He didn't understand what was happening, where he was going, or why he couldn't stay with Mamaw. As the car pulled onto Hwy. 80 he looked back and couldn't bear to watch Mamaw fade out of sight as they drove away. In a single afternoon the world as he had known it—collapsed.

In the car his Mom was smoking and using bad language, something Mamaw never did because she was a preacher and loved Jesus. In the front she seemed to glare at him in the rear view mirror.

Huddled in the back of the car he squeezed his tiny arms around his legs, closed his eyes as hard as he could, and prayed as Mamaw had taught him. He prayed for Mamaw, or someone, to rescue him. But as the sun set in the west Texas sky he realized his prayers were not going to be answered today.

Coming to terms with the tough times of our lives is not fun. It is far different than sitting around and just moaning about one's past. There is a clear difference between trying to learn something from the lessons of the past versus having a lifelong pity-party.

Please believe me that I am not trying to be disrespectful of your pain. I truly understand that your pain may be excruciating. But we are talking about two different responses to the pain of our lives. One is constructive—one is not. One brings about healing—the other causes our wounds to fester. Having gone through both of these responses—let me share my experience with you.

Oddly enough the process began as a result of a homicide investigation I was involved in. In 1998, while a District

Attorney Investigator, I became peripherally involved in a case concerning the disappearance of two young women attending a local college.

First, a pretty young college co-ed disappeared walking home from a local restaurant late at night. Blood was found on a bridge near her home. A massive search began, but was unsuccessful in locating her.

A few weeks later, in early 1999, another co-ed from the same university disappeared from her home. Police found signs of forced entry, a struggle and that someone had been injured. The community's fear was palpable.

After weeks of tireless efforts by the investigative team, the chance of finding the young women appeared to be fading. One day, purely by "chance," I picked up a book entitled, *Talking to Heaven*, by James Van Praagh. I had not heard of Mr. Van Praagh and had no idea what type of work he did. I began to read the book and was strangely intrigued by the stories he told of being able to communicate with those who had passed to the other side.

Now let me interject to say that up to this point in my life I was a typical cop. Conservative political views, things were "cut & dried," black and white, logical not mystical, etc., etc. On top of this, having been raised in a Pentecostal church— all this stuff was pure voodoo to me.

However, by the time I finished the book, almost without putting it down, I thought perhaps Van Praagh could in *some way* help us find the missing girls. I was not convinced of Van Praagh's claims but I was willing to keep an open mind and look into it further.

The next day I told my boss I had an absolutely crazy idea but one worth trying because nothing else seemed to be working in our attempts to find the girls. Cops are notorious for debunking the ability of psychics to solve crimes, find bodies, etc. Although police from time to time use psychics, most do not provide useful information. I was aware of this. I suggested however that we contact Van Praagh to see if he could help.

As I was already scheduled to meet with the FBI in Los Angeles to discuss a couple of homicides I was working on, I thought I could track down Mr. Van Praagh and ask for his help.

My boss, an incredibly talented and respected investigator, gave me the OK. However, before I left for Los Angeles, the investigative team was able to uncover new leads and both young women were located. They had been kidnapped, murdered and buried at the home of a California prison parolee who now sits on death row as a result.

Although this should have ended my journey, it actually resulted in a thirst for knowledge of the spiritual, *not necessarily religious*, aspects of our lives. I began to read more and more about how our lives are divinely created with a specific purpose in mind. I learned that during each of our lifetimes, there are lessons we are meant to learn. In order to learn these lessons, certain events must occur. What I came to realize was that the pain, adversity and challenges we experience in life serve as a means to help us learn those lessons.

Armed with this understanding, I began to examine my own life closely in order to understand why I had experienced so many painful, challenging events. What were the lessons I was meant to learn? How had my painful experiences set the stage to teach me the lessons I needed to learn? I'm here to tell you folks, that *"digging up bones"* is not pleasant, and I had many bones to unearth.

In Phase One, which was the most painful, I spent a great deal of time and quiet contemplation regarding the painful events and times of my life. At times I could almost feel the pain, literally & physically, that I had experienced at the time of the various incidents.

I recalled many frightened times as a child. I could close my eyes and hear my mother's voice in my mind, berating me, cursing about one thing or another. I could picture her hitting me, of her verbal abuse and just plain meanness. I could feel the tension in the home, the arguments between my mother and step-father.

I recalled so many lonely times when I would wander around feeling hopeless, trapped and unloved. I guess that is why during my career as a cop I have had so much empathy for children in bad homes. I know how they feel.

After I had exorcised the "demons" of my past the process evolved into Phase Two. In this phase, I tried to "connect the dots" and find a relationship between the pain of the past and my present personality, biases, strengths and weaknesses, etc. How had the past shaped who I had become?

I realized the hardened exterior and attitude was my defense mechanism and wall to the world. I began to under-stand that my endless pursuit of love in relationships and one night stands was my attempt to find love and acceptance.

Howerer I also began to realize that much of the pain in my life had actually made me stronger than I might have become in the otherwise sheltered, nurturing and "spoiled" environment with Mamaw.

The hard work and mountain of chores piled on us as kids, and long hours of work on the ranch instilled in me a strong work ethic which has been beneficial to me throughout my life. If there's one thing I am not afraid of—it's hard work.

Toward the end of this process I s-l-o-w-l-y began to actually *appreciate* some of the tough times in my life, realizing the lessons they had taught me. I began to agree with the old adages, *"What doesn't kill you only makes you stronger,"* and *"Every painful or difficult time in your life is God's way of giving you an opportunity to grow."*

Having come to terms with my past, Phase Three then became a process of understanding the concept of synchronicity or serendipity—that *"everything happens for a reason"* perhaps if only in hindsight. I know some people feel that as free beings we create our lives, the good times and the bad, through choice. The belief that there are no accidents in life is therefore controversial.

In my case however, looking back over my life I can point to specific incidents, that had they not occurred would have dramatically changed the course of my life. Most were incidents I consciously did not think about at the time. I'm sure if you examined your life you would find the same examples.

In reality however, the events were not coincidental at all, rather the concept of synchronicity at work. In the past few years I have read various books describing "coincidental events" in people's lives. One of the most interesting of these books is entitled, *"There are No Accidents,"* by Robert H. Hopcke. He describes how noted psychiatrist Carl Jung coined the term "synchronicity" for those *"odd, haunting coincidences that we all experience—those moments when events seem to conspire to tell us something, to teach us, to turn our lives around."*

I have a very good friend who went to a local real estate office *on the spur of the moment* to take care of some personal business. He was planning on going another day but had some time so he popped in.

The paperwork he was to pick up was not ready so he walked across the street to a local cafe to kill some time. Lying on the sidewalk in front of the café was a cute little dog which Jeff knelt down to pet. At that moment a gal came around the corner to enter the restaurant, did not see Jeff and almost tripped over him. They both laughed and began to chat about the dog and wound up going in for a cup of coffee together. Today they live together, are talking of marriage, have many mutual interests, and often laugh about the "coincidence" of their first encounter.

If Jeff had went to the real estate office at another time or day he would not have met Linda, as he did not frequent the cafe. Merely a coincidence—or was it "meant to be"? I'll let you decide.

My point is, there are situations like this which happen in all our lives and many are, in my opinion, divinely "meant to be." As I journeyed through Phase Three reflecting on the many "coincidences" of my life, I began to realize that everything in my life had happened for a reason or had a purpose. I was able to specifically identify those situations and incidents in my life, as tough as they were that had taught me a valuable lesson and moved me along my journey.

Had they not occurred I would not have learned the lesson needed at the time, or brought me to the very place I am today. I challenge you to look back on your life and "connect the dots" to find the lessons in the adversity of your life.

CHAPTER 3

House of Pain

Finally arriving at the place he would call home for the next few years, the little boy walked into the small wood-framed ranch house not far from Weatherford, Texas. It was not clean like Mamaw's, and there was a smell in the air. He walked through the house, feeling out of place and afraid. From the familiarity and security of life with Mamaw, to a house of strangers and fear in a matter of hours. Although they were family, he didn't know them.

His stepfather was the ranch foreman of the large cattle ranch and dairy farm. He was taken to the barn and shown around. He would spend many hours there, feeding and milking cows, and cleaning stalls.

As night fell, the stranger called Jean led him to a back bedroom, and said, "This is where you'll sleep" and walked away. He laid in bed and looked out the window towards heaven and the stars. They looked close enough to touch.

He waited for someone to come and kiss him goodnight the way Mamaw had—but no one came. No one made sure he had taken a bath and put on clean pajamas. Lying on his back he closed his eyes and once again prayed for rescue. "Maybe this time it will work," he thought as he fell asleep.

"Time to get up!" his stepfather said. Dairy cows are milked every day of the year at 3:00 a.m. and 3:00 p.m., and he would be at most. He crawled out of bed, wiped his eyes, got dressed and headed for the barn.

As time went on and hope for rescue faded, the barn became his refuge, working and hiding from his mother. On cold winter mornings, he would huddle in the feed room on top of burlap feed bags to sleep. Mice, always a problem, would often wake him as they scurried about, over and under the feed bags. Later, he would use the barn as a secret place to hide the cigarettes he had stolen from his Mom.

For those of you who have lived in a "house of pain" I'm sure you can relate to the little boy's story. As a patrol officer, investigator and Detective Bureau Commander, I have walked through more than my share of violent homes.

Whether the violence was physical or emotional, the result was the same. I can't count the number of times I've had to coax children out of their "hiding spot" in the back of a closet, or from under a bed—their way of escaping the scary times when Mom & Dad were fighting. Seeing them huddled in a corner, their tiny hands cupping their ears to drown out the screaming was heart-wrenching.

Sadly, I often returned time after time over the years and watched as these same kids grew up and became abusive parents themselves. Many wound up in serious trouble with the law.

As an investigator, I have sat with children as they recounted horrible stories of being molested, of physical and emotional abuse. Images of their stories would creep into my dreams and haunt me over and over again.

If you have been the victim of any of this type of abuse, or raised in a home where violence was common, my heart goes out to you. But there is a ray of sunshine to be drawn from these terrible events. Believe it or not there may have been a purpose to it all.

As I've said, I truly believe everything happens for a reason, and that everyone who comes into our lives—does so for a reason. Certain situations occur to shape us into who we are today, and teach us important lessons necessary for personal growth.

Absent these events we would not learn the lessons meant for us. I'm sure you can look back on specific situations in your life that have brought about great change in you and made you stronger or wiser. I'll bet most if not all of those situations were tough times not fun times. I have certainly learned much more from the adversity of my life than from joyous events or occassions.

The problem is most of us do not use the difficult times in our lives to learn or grow. We are too busy trying to get over things, put things behind and move on. This is both good and bad. It is good to have enough strength to overcome adversity—but only after we have examined the event and found the lessons within. It is only then that we can truly put things behind us. If we move forward too quickly we tend to "bury the past" not "learn from it." As a result sooner or later the past returns to hurt us again.

In my current assignment I deal with prison inmates on a daily basis. Many have been in prison for years convicted of murder, rape, robbery, etc. The majority are members of prison and street gangs and have had no positive role models in their lives. Most come from dysfunctional families, some from families where literally every member of the family— father, mother, brothers, and sisters, are gang members and have been in prison at one time or another. Generations of families involved in gangs, crime and jail.

Many of these inmates have not dealt with their past. Instead of finding healing for their wounds they lashed out in anger in one way or another at society.

Interestingly, "some" of these same inmates now have kids of their own and even from a prison cell they "ride herd" on them. They tell of their sons and daughters getting good grades in school, going to college, helping Mom, etc. Ironically, despite their crimes, and the fact they are in prison, some have become positive role models for their children because they don't want their kids to end up where they are.

In talking with older inmates, rarely have I had them brag about their lives and choices. Many say they are ashamed for their actions and realize now that what they thought was "cool" back then, was in fact stupid, selfish, and mean. Peer pressure, drugs, alcohol or gangs got most of them in trouble.

Most tell almost the same story of getting to a certain point where nothing seemed to be working for them. Frustrated or feeling like they could not fix things, they simply gave up and sank forever into a pit they felt they could not crawl out of.

CHAPTER 4

Living in Fear

During the school year, following the morning milking, the little boy would race home from the barn, eat breakfast, get dressed and catch the school bus in front of the ranch. School was a refuge for him. It was a place to play. Yet even at school he was different. Kids would sometimes laugh at him for the clothes he wore, because they were not always clean or didn't fit right. But it was better than being at home.

The worst part of the school day came after lunch because he knew the bell would soon ring, he would board the bus, and return home to his mother. He could not understand where his mother's anger came from. What could have happened to make someone just plain mean? Later in life he would hear rumors about abuse she may have suffered as a child, her alcohol and drug use, and the string of bad relationships with men. Her current marriage was no different.

His mom and stepfather fought constantly about one thing or another. During these periods he and his sister, would sometimes be locked away in the back bedroom of the small farmhouse so they could not have contact with "his" kids, as his mother called her husband's children.

From the window he would stare out at passing cars and trucks on Hwy. 180 wondering where they were going. Maybe if he could get to the road someone would take him with them. At this point he didn't care where—just away from here.

Living in fear is one of the worst things for a person to experience. Fear puts a knot in your stomach, causes sleepless nights, and the anxiety of not knowing what's coming next, keeps one on edge all the time. Living in fear is different than a single fearful moment or experience. Imagine the worst fear of your life and how you would feel if you had to face that situation twenty-four hours a day, seven days a week, year in and year out.

I have dealt with victims of domestic violence during my career who describe this type of fear. Women who lived each day in constant fear of "the next time." For those of you who have been in these types of relationships you know exactly what "the next time" means.

Fear can eat away at one's mental, emotional and physical health. Nervous breakdowns, ulcers, complete loss of self-esteem are all examples of what fear can do to a person.

Children raised in a fearful environment show the effects of it in different ways. Some become extremely introverted, "afraid of their own shadow," and allow themselves to be abused throughout their life.

The fear that grips them is greater than their desire or ability to fight back. I have seen children who begin to shake anytime an adult's voice raises in frustration or anger—even if it's not directed at them.

Other children react in a completely opposite way and become sullen, withdrawn and angry. These are the kids who often grow up to become as mean as the parent, sibling, or whomever that caused them so much fear when they were young. Many inmates in prisons were raised in homes where tension, fear, anger, and abuse were a normal part of life. As someone once said, "what goes around—comes around."

There is another kind of fear that grips many lives. It is not a fear based on violence or monsters from without. It is a fear from within. A secret fear that some of the most powerful folks in America have struggled to overcome.

It is a fear embedded in our minds, perhaps created by significant or seemingly insignificant events during our lives, as children, teenagers or adults.

The fear of not being good enough, not deserving enough, not pretty enough, or smart enough. But I am here to tell you that you are more special, unique and beautiful than you realize.

Consider this. Today's world population exceeds many billions of people. From one end of the earth to the other, at this very moment there are B-I-L-L-I-O-N-S of folks going about their daily tasks. From the jungles of Africa to the streets of New York. From Antarctica to the North Pole. From the farmlands of China to the farmlands of America. B-I-L-L-I-O-N-S of people inhabit our world.

But each person, including YOU, is unique and different and special

In all the world there is *only one you*. You are the *only* person in the world with your fingerprints. You are the *only* person in the world with the same lip prints or retinal pattern. *No one* else laughs exactly like you, smiles like you, cries like you. *No one* else in the entire world has suffered and learned from their experiences exactly like you. You truly are unique in all the world. And the gift inside you is unique also.

It has been blessed with your wisdom and perspective and *can only be shared with others "uniquely" by you.*

Many things have sculpted your gift. Fear, anger, grief, disappointment, betrayal, pain, sadness, loneliness, frustration, or perhaps self-doubt. In other words—your gift is the adversity of your life.

Sharing Your Gift

For those of you who have survived the terror of domestic violence—there are women's shelters and crisis centers who would love to have your help in guiding others who are going through the same things you went through?

You may have had a loved one suddenly taken from you by senseless gang violence and know firsthand the grief, anger, lonliness and frustration this brought to your family. There are hundreds of anti-gang and victim advocacy groups desperately searching for help from people just like you.

You may have been one who has survived and overcame the humiliation, anger and shame of being sexually assaulted, as a child or adult. There are others who need your unique insight and support. You can make a big difference in their lives simply by sitting and holding their hand while they walk through that same valley of darkness and despair? Rape crisis centers are always in need of volunteers.

If you've been awakened during the night screaming over the images of death on the battlefield you have a lot to offer your fellow veterans.

If during your life you fought and won the battle to get the claws of the drug monkey off your back you have an invaluable gift and perspective to share with others who are suffering the same disease. AA and Alanon groups need your help.

Perhaps you have endured the fear, pain and agony of cancer, or some other horrible disease—what have you done to help out in a support group or one on one with someone going through your nightmare?

You see we all have more to offer than we think. We all have *walked through the fire*, so to speak, and have valuable experiences to share.

Have you ever seen programs on television of people who had an unusual disease or problem and how they thought they were the only person in the world with that particular problem? They speak of the agony of thinking they were completely alone—only to find out they weren't and how it changed their world, and gave them hope.

CHAPTER 5

Rescue

One day they moved from the ranch to a home near Ft. Worth, Texas. Although it was a larger house, the little boy still could not find a place to hide from his mother—and he was beginning to change.

Surrounded by alcohol, fighting, and cursing, the pleasant boy was becoming what he hated so—his mother. He started hanging around neighborhood boys and together they cussed, smoked and talked about dirty things. He tried to keep up an image of being tough like them. But at night as he lay in bed he remembered to say his prayers, asking God to forgive him for the things he did that day. As always he still prayed for someone to rescue him as he had every day since he last saw Mamaw. He prayed also for Mamaw not to worry about him or be sad.

His mother seemed to get worse. Tension and fighting in the home was constant and this brought out the worst in his mother. Alcohol was eating her alive.

Then one summer day out of no where—just like the day his mother took him away, an aunt and uncle appeared at the door. They announced he and his sister Pat, were going with them to California. Could this be? He couldn't believe what he was hearing. He wasn't sure what it would be like but he didn't care. He just wanted out of this nightmare.

There was nothing to pack. What little clothes the boy had were not worth taking. Aunt Ruby said they would get him new clothes in California. As they pulled out of the driveway he looked back at the house of pain, but did not wave at the stranger called Jean. Instead he bowed his head and thanked God for finally answering his prayers, even if it had taken too many years.

To the little boy, now twelve, this was only a rescue—the healing would take many more years.

What we all have to learn at some point in our lives is that "rescue" from our tormentors or circumstances involves much more than a physical change in scenery or circumstances. The best and most dramatic "rescue" comes from within.

There are examples of those who, while imprisoned in Nazi death camps during World War II, still managed to remain positive. Stories abound of those who decided that although they endured horrific torture and abuse, they came to terms with their past and "rescued" their souls.

One such example is Henri Landwirth who was just 13 when World War II broke out. Separated from his family, over the next five years he was moved from one labor camp to another, and then to the infamous Auschwitz concentration camp.

In his book, *Gift of Life,* he describes his experiences and how he "saw, heard and experienced man's inhumanity to man firsthand." Somehow, *(perhaps by "chance"),* he survived, but was blinded by hatred.

He made it to America and after a successful career in hotel management turned his energies to helping grant the last wishes of children with terminal illnesses. Along with others in the hotel industry he created "Give Kids the World" a village at Disney World where children with terminal illnesses, and their families stay for free. You see Mr. Landwirth had a choice—to remain blinded by hatred or reach out to love. He chose love and has changed many lives.

One of the most respected women in America today who many of us settle in to watch every day on television, suffered tremendous shame, anger, and humiliation as a child. Not only from racism but sexual abuse as well. But Oprah Winfrey, like Henri Landwirth, had a choice.

A choice to remain imprisoned by her pain—or fight back. She chose to fight back. Her courage to do so, to recreate herself, has been an inspiration to tens of thousands of men and women across America. Today, her show and the Angel Network are helping others triumph as she has.

In my own experience, my "rescue" came about only after I made a conscious decision to face the past and all of it's issues. Issues of abandonment, of feeling unloved, of cruelty suffered at the hands of those who were supposed to love and protect me, of feeling all alone in the world.

Each of these "issues" had its own special affect on my life. Each caused me to do certain things, think certain ways, shield myself in certain ways, blocking out the very love, acceptance and help I had always wanted. When I finally realized what I had been doing to sabotage my own happiness, I began to find a way to crawl out of the darkness.

And when I did folks, I could never imagine how bright the sun was going to shine. The past is nothing but memories. It is not tangible and can not harm you. It is not the "boogie-man," only memories of the "boogie-man." The only power your past has over you is the power you give it. When you release the pain, sorrow, anger or whatever that eats at you from your past—you are truly free. Now YOU have the power, not the past.

CHAPTER 6

Moving On

Life in California with his aunt & uncle was so different from the life he had been living. Aunt Ruby and Uncle Lester did not fight like his Mom and Step Dad did. He was once again going to church regularly. For a few months he was constantly afraid she would come back for him, and he swore to himself he would never go back. At night he prayed as he always had. But now he prayed for God to let him stay in his new home.

Some habits stay with you and the hard work as a boy on the ranch instilled in him a strong work ethic. He quickly found himself a series of jobs. He shined shoes every Saturday at Rick's Barber Shop. He cleaned kitchens for old folks and mowed lawns.

As he grew into a young man he became a leader within the church youth group. Bible quiz team captain, choir member, and leader of the Royal Rangers. He tried to forget the past, to move on with his life but an open wound was festering in his soul. Unbeknownst to others a wound full of anger and resentment, was lying quietly in his soul. He smiled and seemed not to have a care in the world. But the wound was open and bleeding.

A lifetime of moving had caused a constant sense of restlessness. Graduating half way through his senior year he joined the Air Force with an urge to move on. The war in Vietnam was raging and the patriotic young man felt it was his duty to do his part. Military service however became a period of dark bars and alcohol more than anything, and both soon became a major part of his life.

But in this environment he felt safe. He could pretend to be someone he was not, and bury it all—and the past—in the bottom of a bottle. The void in his life was growing but he didn't know how to fill it.

If you're like me, you've probably sat on a beach, a hilltop or other quiet, calm place wondering, "Why am I here?" You may have felt a strange void in your soul. For many years I could not figure out why I felt this way or how to fill the void. It was hard for me to "move on" with my life because of the emptiness in my soul.

Perhaps you thought a perfect relationship with "Mr. or Ms. Right" would fill the void. Maybe it was that perfect job, home or money in the bank. Some of you may have instead decided to bury your void in drugs, alcohol or some other destructive behavior.

Do you remember a few years ago, a fast food commercial depicting a elderly gray-haired lady standing in line looking down at her hamburger asking, "WHERE'S THE BEEF?"

Where's the "beef" in your life? Has the "beef" for you been climbing the corporate ladder; improving your resume; accumulating more than your parents had; traveling in the right social circles; being a member of this group or that country club; or keeping up with the Jones'? And if so—as Dr. Phil asks: "How's that been working for you?"

Sarah Ban Breathnach in her book, *Something More* said, *"Money, marital status, fame, admiration and accomplishment mean nothing if the soul is starving."*

Is your soul starving? If so, it may be that you have not yet discovered how to feed your soul. Until a few short years ago I too was searching for "the beef" in my life. Running at full speed on the corporate treadmill, I was in search of success and fulfillment. My corporate ladder was different than most of you however. Mine was law enforcement.

From Patrol Officer to Detective, Hostage Negotiator, Sergeant and Detective Bureau Commander, I climbed the ladder. Manager of this, manager of that, board member of this, committee member of that. Always trying to improve my resume.

But my soul was starving

My office walls were covered with plaques and awards. Officer of the Year, Certificate for Valor & Bravery, Distinguished Service Awards, Commendation Certificates. Even an award from the California State Assembly for excellence and leadership as a Detective Bureau Commander.

But my soul was starving

An upward climb to the elite Bureau of Investigation for the District Attorney's Office. Up and up I climbed eventually becoming a candidate for U.S. Congress. Rubbing elbows with the high & mighty & wealthy—even the President of the United States.

But my soul was starving

Through all these years, I was given many opportunities to learn my life's lessons. However, blinded by ambition I did not. It took many years to understand that what I was searching for was not success but—acceptance.

I believe the purpose of our lives is not found in who we are professionally, what social circles we run in, or what we achieve and accumulate. It is not found in the car we drive, or the home we own.

Now don't get me wrong. I'm not advocating moving to a camel camp in the desert, or a commune in the woods. I'm not saying ambition or a desire to improve yourself professionally or economically is wrong. *I'm just saying that when it becomes your primary focus in life—it may be time to examine your priorities.*

Charles Schultz, the creator of Snoopy and Charlie Brown had a great philosophy about life and it centers around the following "life quiz."

1. Name the five wealthiest people in the world.
2. Name the last five Heisman trophy winners.
3. Name the last five winners of the Miss America contest.
4. Name ten people who have won the Nobel or Pulitzer Prize.

5. Name the last half dozen Academy Award winners for best actor and actress.

6. Name the last decade's worth of World Series winners.

How did you do? The point is, none of us remember the headliners of yesterday, those who have accumulated the most, scored the most points or even found cures for diseases.

These are no second-rate achievers. They are the best in their fields. But the applause dies. Awards tarnish. Achievements are forgotten. Accolades and certificates are buried with their owners.

Now take this quiz and see how you do:

1. List a few teachers who aided your journey through school.

2. Name three friends who have helped you through a difficult time.

3. Name five people who have taught you something worthwhile.

4. Think of a few people who have made you feel appreciated and special.

5. Think of five people you enjoy spending time with.

6. Name half a dozen heroes whose stories have inspired you.

A little easier? I thought so. The lesson is obvious—*The people who make a difference in your life are not the ones with the most credentials, the most money, or the most awards. They are the ones that care.*

I believe one of the primary purposes in life is to do whatever we can to benefit mankind. To show compassion for others. To bring hope to others. To help guide others through the tough times of their lives. It does not mean you can't strive to be the best you can be. It simply means a part of you has been specifically set aside to help others.

Perhaps you're not certain how you can help. You may think, "I'm not smart enough, talented enough, or rich enough to help. I don't have a degree or a fancy title." Perhaps you have had problems in your life. Bills, the law, job problems, marital problems—on and on. **ALL THESE THINGS DO NOT MATTER.**

What matters is your willingness to help. Your willingness to abandon the past, and start down a new road that creates a new history for you. There are s-o-o-o-o many examples of people who have been in horrible places in their lives, but due to the power of a simple choice dramatically changed their lives and destiny, and went on to change the world. Now your time has arrived.

CHAPTER 7

The Gift Discovered

The young man grew into a man. Joining the service at an early age he was finally on his own. He was now free to find true happiness in his own way.

His search however was ill conceived. He believed he could find love and acceptance in relationships—but he was afraid because down deep, the little boy still felt unworthy of love.

Through bars and the nightlife of every town he lived in or traveled to, the man found only emptiness.

Despite his fear he finally married and tried to raise a family, but alas this too faded away. His work brought great but empty success. His search for happiness seemed endless. He tried marriage again but that too failed.

In desperation he finally realized he was searching in the wrong places. Instead of looking to others for happiness, or striving for greater professional success to make him feel worthy—he discovered true happiness and a sense of self-worth very close to home—within himself.

One Christmas evening a phone call he never thought would come—did. It was his Mom, Jean the stranger. Although now a grown man and police officer, he suddenly felt the fear he had as a little boy. As he heard her speak he wanted to interrupt and tell her how bad she had hurt him, how cruel and mean she had been, and even how much he had wanted her to love him.

His mother began to cry and apologize for all the bad things she had done. She asked for his forgiveness and told him, "I love you son." After all the years that had passed, these words sank deep into his heart and without thinking he replied, "I love you too Mom—please don't cry." It would be the last time he spoke to her as she died shortly thereafter, her body ravaged by the life she had lived.

The little boy who had grown into a man hating the mother who gave him birth, now forgave her and offered her love. It had been a long journey but somewhere along the way the little boy had found a gift that made the journey worthwhile.

Today my journey is over and I am no longer angry with God, or life or Mom.

You see folks, like you I too have been given a gift and have tried to share it with you. My prayer for you is that you will find the gift within yourself, be good to yourself, because, like me you've done the best you could do at the time—whether it was or not.

Although my two beautiful daughters do not know it, I have agonized over my mistakes as a father. I could have been more loving, less strict, more understanding, spoiled them more. And on and on it goes. Hindsight is always 20-20. As the years go by all I can do is let them both know how much I love them and be the best father I can be every day of the year for the rest of my life.

Whether it was raising our children, failed relationships, personal challenges, we have all made mistakes. It's time to forgive yourself and move on. Each of us has suffered in our own ways. Life at times has seemed unfair to us. That's what I thought for years. As I said before, it doesn't matter what caused the pain in your life—pain is <u>pain and it hurts.</u>

Perhaps you have allowed the pain of your life to rule you. But no more. Now is the time to begin your journey to healing. What I discovered was that healing was something I had to accept and allow into my life. <u>It won't force itself into</u> <u>your life. You have to invite it in. Your willingness to allow</u> <u>healing into your life is a powerful step.</u>

When I did, it seemed as though the universe opened the skies of heaven and wrapped me in love. I found a tremendous amount of strength coming to me in the process, because for once in my life—I was in control—not the circumstances of my life. In this process I also had to forgive myself—just as you must.

Like me folks, you may now be at a crossroad in your life and the time has come to make a decision. A decision to move on, to heal & forgive—or continue to rot away from the inside out. If you don't your life may never be all it can truly be.

In order to forgive we must set our ego aside, and that is not always easy to do. I remember as part of my journey I reached a point where my ego needed a strong dose of medicine. Having been in management and investigative positions in law enforcement for so many years, I thought I was "all that." And then the universe conspired to teach me a lesson.

Having quit my job in law enforcement to run for Congress, I was stunned to find myself defeated in the race and my marriage collapsing all at the same time. Suddenly I was unemployed, going through a divorce and basically homeless. What had happened to my life?

Luckily I was able to quickly find a job as a ranch hand at a local ranch and moved into "bunk" quarters. For a few months I worked from sun up to sun down on the ranch. Was it a "coincidence" that I had found this job at this particular time in my life? Although the work was long, hot and hard—working with the horses was just what the doctor ordered. Hauling horses around the state gave me an opportunity to "clear my head" and reestablish priorities in life.

After a few months I accepted an oil field job as a roustabout. My ego had a sudden jolt when on the first day I found myself working side by side with parolees from prison. I was responsible for sending some of them to prison as a result of my investigations. Talk about a strange situation. The worst part was that I somehow felt so embarrassed to be working in the same place with them. What were they thinking about me?

 This experience turned out to be very good for me in that each day more and more of my ego was stripped away. When I returned to law enforcement a short time later I vowed never again to take things for granted.

So how strong is your ego? Is it preventing you from forgiving—from letting go of the past?

Cesar Chavez, the famous labor leader once said, *"When we are really honest with ourselves we must admit our lives are all that really belong to us. So it is how we use our lives that determines the kind of men and women we are."*

I challenge you to examine your life and ask yourself what kind of a man or woman you are. Then make a decision to forgive yourself if you must, to discover your gift and find a way you can share your gift with others. Then go out and set the world on fire.

Author Zora Neale Hurston said, *"There is no agony like bearing an untold story inside you."*

Your story is waiting to be shared so don't let it go untold. You never know the miracle you can create in someone's life.

APPENDIX

Heroes Among Us

There are many heroes in the world today. Some you are familiar with, others you are not. These are people who have turned the adversity in their lives into a powerful force for good. They have reached out and shared their *"gift"* with others and the world is a better place because of it.

Some of these heroes have suffered the loss of a loved one as you have. Death may have taken a spouse, a son or daughter, mother or father, dear friend or lover from you. You may have sat and watched the life slowly drain out of them. Just as a soldier on the battlefield watching a buddy die, you too know this same sense of helplessness. Perhaps a loved one was suddenly taken from you. Each loss can cause the pain and grief to be almost palpable.

As a police officer and investigator, I have witnessed scores of deaths. Homicides, suicides, traffic accidents, crib deaths, and others. I have sat with families of murder victims and witnessed the devastation of their lives when something so senseless occurs.

I have had to deliver the ominous message in the middle of the night to parents that a child of theirs has been tragically taken from them. As a father myself, this was always very difficult.

ANGER/HATRED

I doubt there is anyone who has not heard of M.A.D.D.—Mothers Against Drunk Drivers. In 1980, Candy Lightner was the proud mother of a beautiful 13-yr. old daughter—when a drunk driver suddenly took her daughter from her. There is nothing worse than a parent experiencing the loss of a child. The anger and grief Candy felt was devastating. But Candy made a choice. Rather than succumb to the anger and grief she made a choice. A choice to fight back—and not let her daughter's death be in vain.

Along with other women she founded M.A.D.D. and by 1982 M.A.D.D. had grown to over 100 chapters. President Reagan announced the formation of a Presidential Task Force on Drunk Driving and invited M.A.D.D. to serve on it.

By 1984, M.A.D.D. had over 350 chapters nationwide and had ventured into Canada as well. M.A.D.D. continues to grow and has chapters throughout the world. All of this from a simple choice by a very courageous lady.

Our home is our sanctuary and that was what Leslie Douglass Frizell thought of the Oklahoma home she shared with her parents and brother. At least that is what she thought before two crazed men invaded their home in 1979. Two men, Steven Keith Hatch and Glen Ake, raped her, murdered her parents, then in a final act shot her and her brother at point blank range, before fleeing the home. But both she and her brother survived the horrible ordeal. Both men were later arrested, convicted and sentenced to death.

It took many years for the wheels of justice to turn but finally in 1996 Steven Hatch was executed by lethal injection. Leslie attended his execution hoping that by witnessing the process it would finally give her a sense of closure and peace from the anger she had felt for so long. But this was not to be. She left the prison with as much poison in her soul as when she entered.

This continued until Leslie reached a point where she realized that in order to be an example to her children and move on with her life, she had to find forgiveness in her heart for these men. She described the process of "forgiving" as one of freedom for her. Freedom from the bitterness and anger that had been eating away at her for so many years. Her brother's story is similar.

Brooks "Chip" Douglass grew up to become a state senator from Oklahoma. Although Steven Hatch's conviction and death sentence was upheld, the other subject, Glen Ake, had the death-penalty portion of his conviction overturned. In 1986, Glen Ake was sentenced to two life terms in prison.

On impulse, during a legislative tour of the prison where Ake was being held, Douglass asked to meet him. It was roughly a year before Hatch's execution.

For 90 minutes they talked face to face, separated by the visiting-room panel of glass. Both cried most of the time. Ake said he was very sorry for what he had done. Douglass said that for 16 years he had wanted nothing more than to see Ake dead.

Then Douglass said he was tired of being bitter and angry. He got up and started to walk out, then turned around, went back to the glass, and told Glen Ake he forgave him.

"I could almost see this poison flowing out of me all over the floor. It was like I hadn't taken a breath in 16 years, and suddenly I could breathe again," says Douglass. You see Chip Douglas made a simple choice and his life changed forever.

DIVORCE

I'm sure there are many of you, like myself, who have suffered the tremendous sense of sadness, guilt, anger, and failure as a result of divorce. Sadly in America today, the divorce rate hovers around 65%. The average marriage in our nation has a life span of 19 months. I have felt the sting of divorce twice in my life.

My first marriage lasted many years and the toughest day of my life was walking out the door of our home. The night before I told my youngest daughter that Daddy was leaving. The next morning I awoke to find a note she had slid under the door of my bedroom. A note she had sat and written all alone, in the quiet of her room after our talk.

"Dear Daddy, No matter what you decide I want you to know that I'm proud of you and think you're a good person. I know you will do the right thing. Wherever you are, we will always be best buddies. Love, Angela."

I don't know about you, but at that moment I felt like the absolute worst father in the world. How could I walk out of her life? How could I be so selfish?

My oldest daughter had already left home when the divorce occurred but I'm sure it's affect on her was just as painful. Our relationship was very rocky for some time and it continues to heal today. She will never know the amount of love I have for her. All I can do is continue to show my love for her and rebuild the bridges that time, and pride and ego helped to erode.

I continued to feel bad about the pain I caused my ex-wife despite the passage of time so I sat down and wrote her a letter a few years after the divorce. I thanked her for what she had brought to my life and apologized for any pain I had ever caused her. I never heard back from her but that was not what I was looking for. I had done my part and reached out to perhaps help her wounds heal.

For those of you who have been there, you understand exactly what I'm talking about. From the agony of my divorce I learned many lessons and have since spent time with friends going through the same thing, trying to help them overcome the anger, pain and sadness of the death of their family.

CHILD ABUSE

Sadly some of you are victims of child abuse. The form it took does not matter. Whether it was physical, emotional, or sexual in nature the pain is the same. During my years with my mother I came face to face with physical and emotional abuse. I know what it's like to be locked in a bedroom for days. I have felt the sting of belts across my back and face. I know what it's like to be told and treated as if I was basically worthless. I know what living in fear is all about and I'm sure there are some of you who have suffered the same fate.

One of the most inspirational stories of overcoming the brutality and pain of child abuse is chronicled in a series of books by David J. Pelzer. In his first book, *A Child Called It,* Dave describes the horrible abuse he suffered at the hands of his mother, a mentally disturbed alcoholic. *The Lost Boy,* describes his journey through the foster care system. In *A Man Named Dave* he tells his story of recovery and hope. Finally his latest work entitled *Help Yourself,* Dave tells how to move beyond your painful past, negative thoughts and take control of your life.

Dave Pelzer is now married with a son of his own who has been selected as one of Ten Outstanding Young Americans.

RACISM

I was raised in Texas at a time before the civil rights movement was born. I remember the "whites only" and "colored" bathrooms and drinking fountains. I grew up hearing the "N" word used in hateful, vicious ways. I know what white hooded robes look like. I remember walking down the street as a boy and having grown men who were "colored", as they called them then, look down at the ground and either step off the sidewalk or cross the street allowing a little white boy to go by.

Some of you have felt the venom of racism and bigotry firsthand. You have felt the anger of being treated poorly simply because of your race, ethnicity, or religion. Sadly this is not just an American phenomena. There are people throughout the world devoting their lives to this kind of vile. The ethnic cleansing in Bosnia and Ruwanda are examples of this, as is the hatred of radical Muslim factions that seek the destruction of America and Israel.

How many of us could have withstood the racism and bigotry in the peaceful and dignified manner Dr. Martin Luther King did? A humble southern Baptist minister who made a decision and choice to fight the inequality and viciousness of racism at a time in America when the Klan was alive and well, not just in the small towns and back roads of the south but in the halls of government as well.

Many of you probably remember the police dogs in Selma, Alabama being turned loose on American citizens simply because of the color of their skin. But Dr. King made a decision to fight on, and in doing so helped change the course of American history.

VETERANS

As a combat veteran you may have witnessed the brutality of war. I applaud you for your service to our nation. Perhaps you watched as friends died on the battlefield. The movie "Saving Private Ryan" has been described by some as probably the most graphic depiction of war—but some veterans say even it can not compare with the real thing.

Some of you may have held a buddy in your arms as they drew their last breath, as they cried for their mothers. Perhaps you suffered terrible injuries—physically and emotionally. *Only you* can truly understand the terrible sense of helplessness when the price of war is paid in human lives.

There are many silent heroes among us today. Veterans who have returned from the ravages of war and went on to lead successful lives, raising families and building businesses. Men and women described by Tom Brokaw in his book, *The Greatest Generation.*

There are veterans across America like Republican Sen. John McCain, a Vietnam veteran, who after being shot down was brutalized to the point of death as a POW. The injuries sustained during his ordeal are still with him today. Sen. McCain also made a choice. He chose not to allow his captors to control his life forever. His journey is one of the most amazing stories and politics asides; he has been an inspiration to many veterans in our country.

Democratic Sen. Daniel Inouye of Hawaii paid a great price in war. As a 2nd Lieutenant and platoon leader in E Company, he fought bravely in the battle of Colle Musatello in Northern Italy. On April 21, 1945 he was shot in the stomach and lost his right arm to a grenade blast. Later awarded the Distinguished Service Cross, (which was upgraded to a Medal of Honor), a Bronze Star, and Purple Heart, Sen. Inouye came home a hero.

His battles were not over however. He had a choice to make. Give in to his injuries and disability or go for broke. He went for broke and changed the course of political history in Hawaii. He has proudly served our nation for decades and "done his family proud" as we say in the South.

ILLNESS

I saw an interview show once in which Michael J. Fox the actor was interviewed. As I'm sure you're aware, Michael is suffering from Parkinson's Disease at an unusual early age. The disease has slowly ravaged his body. During the interview he was asked how it had changed his life. His answer made him a hero in my eyes.

He said his life has never been better. Because of his illness he feels he has become a better father and husband, and appreciates life more now than ever before. He has written a wonderful book entitled, *Lucky Man* and tells how he now focuses on the truly important things in life rather than where he'll be able to park his Lamborghini without it getting scratched, or what movie role may or may not come his way.

You see Michael had a choice. To wallow in self-pity and anger, or focus on the beauty of life and his family. His courage, his "GIFT" has inspired countless thousands of people—especially his wife and kids.

SUBSTANCE ABUSE

Perhaps the pain and destruction of substance abuse has touched your life. It may have been, or still is,—a child, spouse, brother or sister, parent or friend. The frustration remains the same. You may feel totally helpless because all your begging, pleading, threatening and tears do nothing to convince them to stop or seek help.

It may be your own personal battle. For those afflicted by this hideous disease, you live with a daily sense of guilt, anger, and shame. It eats at you and you may have given up all hope—but I beg you not to. Whether it's a demon in your gut or monkey or your back—you can do it.

People do overcome addictions and go on to use the experience gained to help others. One such example is Betty Tyson. Today she is free after serving almost 25 years in prison for a crime she did not commit.

At 24 years old, Betty was selling her body and soul on the streets of Rochester, NY to get her next fix. A local businessman was found murdered and through a series of circumstances and haste, police quickly focused on Betty, a local prostitute.

Beaten and handcuffed to a chair for several hours, Betty was forced to confess. A male friend of Betty's suffered the same fate and also confessed. Betty was convicted and sentenced to 25-life, in spite of the fact there was no evidence linking her to the crime.

In 1980 however, the lead detective in the case was found guilty of fabricating evidence in a case. Her lawyer said this didn't apply to Betty and she continued to languish in prison.

During this time however, Betty earned her high-school diploma, counseled other inmates and became a prize-winning photographer. She tried to turn a negative into a positive and did.

In 1997 one of the witnesses who testified against Betty recanted and said he had been jailed and threatened by the lead detective in the case. This caused the case to be reinvestigated and evidence that should have been given to Betty's lawyers in 1973 wound up clearing her name.

In May 1997, Betty Tyson was released from prison. She received a large settlement for her time in prison and continues to help counsel others. Surprisingly, she says of her time in prison that it probably saved her life. "If I'd stayed out in the street, I probably would have ended up dead—killed, overdosed or from AIDS. But I turned a negative into a positive. I found out who Betty Tyson was."

FINANCIAL STRUGGLES

Many of you have suffered through tough financial times in your lives, perhaps you may still be suffering. I can remember once upon a time counting pennies to buy milk for my kids, living from payday to payday, robbing from Peter to pay Paul. There have been times in my life when I didn't want to answer the phone because I knew it was a creditor wanting money I did not have. I have felt the embarrassment and shame of bankruptcy.

Each of these situations show how the common thread of adversity has touched all of our lives. I doubt there is anyone here who has not been affected by one of these scenarios.

Adversity has affected each one of us in different ways. It has changed our lives. Because of it we can all relate to each other better, have greater compassion and empathy for each other, and ultimately love one another as we were meant to do.

The surgeon turned author, Don Miguel Ruiz in his book, *The Mastery of Love* said, *"We can even say that our suffering is a gift. If you just open your eyes and see what is around you, it's exactly what you need to clean your poison, to heal your wounds, to accept yourself—and to get out of hell."*

What are you going to do with your gift? Who better to help others going through any of the circumstances I've talked about, than someone who has been there and back— someone like you? Who better understands and can relate to someone going through these situations than you? If you've been to hell and back you know the way. Someone once said, *"Suffering gives us x-ray vision into the suffering of others."*

Perhaps that is why former addicts are the best substance abuse counselors. Why former prostitutes have the best luck getting other young women off the streets. Why combat veterans do the best job relating to, and helping, other veterans. Why cancer survivors are best equipped to help others stricken with this dreaded disease.

Difficult times and situations make heroes of ordinary people who choose to use the adversity of their lives to recreate themselves and help others. Albert Einstein truly was a brilliant man when he said, *"In the middle of difficulty lies opportunity."*

You may think you can't do it, that it's too painful; too hard. You may feel that you've buried the memories of your past and you just want to keep them buried. I'm here to tell you can do it—you can make a difference. Ralph Waldo Emerson said, *"What lies behind us, and what lies before us are tiny matters, compared to what lies within us."*

By making a decision to use your gift—you will heal the wounds of your past, bury the demons and literally change both your life and the lives of others forever. I believe it is the purpose in each of our lives.

The choice however is yours. The choice to change your mind and do something productive with the lessons you've learned from the adversity of your life.

The Course in Miracles, states, *"The greatest power we have as human beings, is the power to change our minds."*

Think about that for a moment. *"The greatest power we have…is the power to change our minds."*

The writer Dorothy Gillman said, *"It's when we're given choice that we sit down with the Gods and design ourselves."* What design have you made for your life? Maybe it's time for a new design.

We have the power to either continue to be victimized by the trials and tribulations of our lives—or be initiated by them. For those of you who have been victimized by others—you have a choice. Continue to let your victimizer have power over your life—or take back your life.

I've heard that the beautiful feathers of a peacock are created by the peacock eating and digesting thorns. What a beautiful metaphor for the adversity of our lives. Just like the peacock, the harsh things we often must digest in our lives however can also contribute to our beauty.

I have shared many examples of people who have overcome tremendous challenges, trials and tribulations and negotiated the bumps and ruts of life's highway to become masters of their lives—and in so doing changed other lives as well.

But now it's your turn my friend. What are you going to do with your gift? Keep it tucked away in your heart and soul—or share it with the world? Sarah Ban Breathnach once said, *"We'd all like to think that we're insignificant, but the truth is that each one of us has enough power embedded in our being to set the world on fire."*

George Eliot, said *"It is never too late to be what you might have been."*

In a scene from the movie, *The Natural* starring Robert Redford and Glenn Close, Redford is lying in a hospital bed sick and discouraged thinking his baseball career and life itself is over. Glenn Close delivers a brilliant line saying to him, *"We all have two lives—the life we learn with, and the life we live after that."*

The life you have led up to this very day is the life you have *learned with*—now what are you going to do from this day forward with your *life after that.*

You have surely learned from your experiences, from the trials and tribulations, the pain and suffering of your life. But now it's time to *share.* Your adversity has given you an opportunity to impact others as you never felt you could, and make a REAL difference in someone's life.

RESOURCE LITERATURE

FORGIVENESS

Forgiveness is a Choice: A Step by Step process for Resolving Anger and Restoring Hope
Robert D. Enright

How to Forgive When You Can't Forget: Healing Our Personal Relationships
Charles Klein

ADVERSITY

The Power to Prevail: Turning Your Adversities into Advantages
David Foster

Soaring Into the Storm: A Book About Those Who Triumph Over Adversity
Alison Asher

SYNCHRONICITY

Unexpected Miracles: The Gift of Synchronicity and How to Open It
David Richo

Synchronicity & You: Understanding the Role of Meaningful Coincidences in Your Life

Frank Joseph

SUPPORT GROUPS

National Center for Victims of Crime
2000 M Street NW, Suite 480
Washington, D.C. 20036
(202) 467-8700
www.ncvc.org

Gift From Within (International Organization for Survivors
of Trauma and Victimization)
16 Cobb Hill Rd.
Camden, Maine 04843
(207) 236-8858
www.giftfromwithin.org

Divorce Headquarters
www.divorcehq.com

Grief Net
P.O. Box 3272
Ann Arbor, MI 48106
www.griefnet.org

BIBLIOGRAPHY

Breathnacht, Sarah Ban, *Something More*, Warner Books, New York, NY (1998)

Brokaw, Tom, *The Greatest Generation.*, Vintage/Ebury *(Division of Random House)*, New York, NY (2001)

DeAngelis, Barbara, *Unleash Your Passion*, Simon & Schuster, New York, NY (2002)

Fox, Michael, *Lucky Man,* Hyperion Press, New York, NY (2002)

Gillman, Dorothy, *The Course in Miracles,* Foundation for Inner Peace, Mill Valley, Ca. (1975)

Hopcke, Robert H., *There are No Accidents*, New York, NY Riverhead Books, New York, NY (1997)

Landwirth, Henri, *Gift of Life,* Private printing, (1996)

Luskin, Frederic, *Forgive for Good,* San Francisco, Ca. (2003)

Pelzer, David J., *A Child Called It,* Health Communications, Deerfield Beach, FL. (1995)

_____ *The Lost Boy,* Health Communications, Deerfield Beach, FL. (1997)

_____ *A Man Named Dave,* Plume, New York, NY(2000)

_____ *Help Yourself,* Plume, New York, NY (2001)

Ruiz, Don Miguel, *The Mastery of Love,* Amber-Allen Publishing, San Rafael, Ca. (1999)

Smedes, Lewis B., *Forgive and Forget: Healing the Wounds We Don't Deserve,* San Francisco, Harper, (1996)

About the Author

Allen Rowe is a former Detective Bureau Commander, Congressional candidate and author of *The Justice Corner* a weekly newspaper column. He has received awards for valor and leadership. Allen is the father of two grown daughters, Kristi and Angela, and lives in Monterey, Ca. with his wife Clarissa.

Allen enjoys a growing demand for public speaking engagements noted for their generous mix of inspiration, humor, and hope. For further information on booking Allen for your event go to *www.allenrowe.com*. For a list of very inspiring stories of those who have overcome adversity in their lives visit *www.lifechallenges.org*.

0-595-31228-4